A toffee, a tart, a perfect bedlam. A hose splits, it's like a fountain in this brackish lake my day.

My quick lid sits fit
it hits

Sssssssssssk

Wooooooooooooo

Oooooooooommmmmmmm

Llllllllllllliiiiiiiiiiii

Llllllllllllllnnnnnn

Eeeeeeeeooooop

Nnnnnnaaaaaaaaa

The blossoms crashed in on the milkweed.

So in between the chores and meals we began putting on jokes. We had limited material, but we made do.

We broke each other's faces with rash gestures of affection.

What takes the day and makes it gone?

I want things and beautiful
light, a perfectly soft don't.

I have not yet tried screaming.

It'll be a whole thing.

A mountain city of toad splendor.

PUBLISHING GENIUS PRESS
Baltimore, MD

Cover and rocks: Stephanie Barber
www.StephanieBarber.com
Pages: Adam Robinson

www.PublishingGenius.com
www.ToadSplendor.com

ISBN 13: 978-0-9831706-8-6

stories and poems

Megan McShea

Publishing Genius
Baltimore 2013

FIRST PART

SECOND PART

THIRD PART

"What makes you think anyone will understand that?"
Joseph asks.

"I don't worry about that."

"You are playing high and mighty."

"I am telling the truth. Man has been corrupted by his
symbols. Language has killed his animal."

"And you are resurrecting it?"

"No. It has never had an opportunity to live."

"What will you do about it?"

"I shall continue to ask How."

"How to what?"

"To the strange, unborn thing which is in all men."

—*Kenneth Patchen,* The Journal of Albion Moonlight

"Only one word needs to be discovered in order for a
whole language to change. Imperceptible births which
serve us as proof of existence, our liberations of energy,
our coming to the world, our duration more intensely
lived. And one would not write were it not for this birth
of words that gives again the hope of a true life."

—*Yves Bonnefoy, interview with Serge Gavronsky*
***in* Poems and Texts**

FIRST PART

THE BRAIN IS A PLEASURE ORGAN

In a shell, after a rain, cold, bright morning, after a spell, beside likenesses to past women or men, standing, awful and goaded, along a road for passing by, like it's fun, like we stupidly became serious for years and years, after dying, there in the house, pretending it's hard, happy to pretend.

When the warm, after shadows pulled back when the world spins, when the warm drapes the air and the light pours towards us, in a tree, picking leaves, making comparisons, apples and oranges, this that. Smallest sounds, churning & churched, by light, by afterthoughts, plunging and skimming, finding a level path. A likeness of apparitions stands, making its meaning noises. "More words, no god, no more." There it stands, like supper warmed her. Evening closed in again to say again the same words, the same summer, the same spell over and over, like a lark, whoo-ooing, like a mention, murmured in the best time, for a moment, for some sordid afterthought crumbling sight unseen under it all. It was night.

But the weightless light, spilled over the ridge, brings tiny voices, greatness dwindling, a day, likened to a mouth, mouthing something about the brain, about the brain being a pleasure organ.

TABLE SAW

Table
Table saw
Table saw bird
Table saw bird fly
Table saw bird fly out
Table saw bird fly out singing

11 IRRITATIONS THAT MORNING

I want things and beautiful
light, a perfectly soft don't.
It's my 9th most enormous
successful feeling, timed upon an at.
Only I got busy and now, gee,
I don't remember entering
the pleasures, and that elation—
don't scare me. Maybe there
wasn't this dangerous surface.
Maybe there was just the destination,
when a trunk full of minutiae
that scare me are there, and mundane
ideas that scare that death refreshment.
I could bring you until it's dirty again,
and give you things with sparkling horror.
Don't you have a room of culinary experiments
that can sort the bathroom holidays?

On the street, that recently-cleaned texture
of things. To be alone daily makes
everyone seem interesting

SIGHT UNSEEN

A ventricle detonated without any visible cue from the audience.
Made without care, brought without concern, passed without notice.
Apparently my left arm rose between them and I was so embarrassed.
There's a lost architectural term for that. My word.

Things about my feelings were brought before you and you
just were not that brought out about it. Maybe there wasn't much to do.
There was a whole time dimension about it, an atmosphere of waiting.
Maybe you just couldn't wait.

Please is not the word.

I have not yet tried screaming. I have not yet shown anyone the thing I
mean. I have benched it for now. A lovely bench between the rosebushes.

Approaching greatness sideways like ants without eyes.
Apostles to underworld throngs with their horns and their palettes.
Just beckoning horrors
without any friends to reckon with
life speaks about it just however you like
in wild sound or
roused from between your knees
maybe after a light rain.
A bench on another day.

THE APPOINTMENT

The place was flatter than we had imagined it. We thought it would be a squat tower. But we knew it was the right building from all the friendly notes we'd received on how to make-believe, how to drop things dramatically, how to check our pulses. We rang the bell. The intercom, responding, confused us. It sounded like the ocean, but in a very high resolution, with cries of birds and shouts tossed by waves and even sand under our feet. A young, alert woman finally answered the door, holding it open for us and peering around in the street behind us, gesturing for us to enter the warm foyer.

By the time she shut the door, we had already removed most of our clothing. A pack of dogs startled us and then changed into a flock of soldiers, chasing us into the next room, where a plate of lemon bars and a tea service awaited, only, it was made of wax. "This is nothing like I expected," said my mother, who had persuaded me to join her in coming here. "Well, what did you expect?" I asked. "I thought it would be rosy, like a womb." she said. She sounded sad.

"Change your rabbits!" came a shout from up the stairs, and then again, descending closer, "change your rabbits immediately!" A man in coveralls appeared with wide black eyes. "Oh, pardon me," he said when he saw us there. "You're not the people I thought you were."

But it was too late, for mother and I had already changed our rabbits.

YELLING SÉANCE
IN A CROWDED THEATER

Dots gang up on lines in a tiny room, they go into a tiny room then something happens outside the room, and they stop what they were doing and do something different, until they are bigger than the entirety of whatever is outside the room. Then they relax, their dogs relax, their crabs relax, they become oysters and listen. Nearby, the jello salad is a world unto itself, a complexity going unnoticed within this complexity, until now, with the quiet oysters listening. Outside again, making something tall out of something wide, a narrow scaffolding viewed from afar, where the laboring classes are getting agitated about it, taking turns being figure and ground, figure and ground, a groundswell of answers to questions no one has asked yet, and a final, wavering opening, like a tunnel flying. Like they borrowed a picnic and made a brain out of it. Like showing what's going on in five different rooms of a house, and suddenly what's going on is the same in all the rooms, and the house turns into a huge mechanical buzzard and flies off.

Quick lace everywhere, ornamenting silence with a tasteful quick lace everywhere, so a hundred thousand souls can laugh in peace.

BATH TIDES

The gray girl sinks under the surface of the bathwater, singing in her mouth, humming her autobiography for a distant audience. Pause. Applause.

She trips on the broken walkways in Sunday's park of time. Her anguish drips its wax all over her mother's fine end tables. Her hollow thoughts make a duller sound than expected.

For towels, bright lamps wove in bird and space sounds. The decision to dry was not made lightly.

A pounce slides in on its own tough, gristly meat. Maybe this is something new, she thinks. Along the edge of town, a broad green symmetry presents itself, bakes its feet in the hot sun, shakes its huge apple tree. The worms rain down.

It means for towels, bright lamps wove in bird and space sounds. It means the decision to dry was not made lightly.

Her figurative decorations, splayed along her mantels and shelves, got together last week to discuss all this, discuss us. We are like small, hapless oceans, they decided, who drink to your health while secretly evaporating. What we don't realize, they agreed, is that we waste all our energy fighting tides.

It means we have consensus. It means you love me. It means you were never in any danger. It means wake up. It means we are here now. It means we have a few dollars left, a few hours left, a few apples left, etc. It means jump.

You jump now. You send it if you want. I mean light and sounds real light and sounds like lapping, like sun on bathwater.

BALTIMORE PRAYER

Precisely this fogged window, which prevails in the cold, wet night, blinks out onto an uninhabited land of Other People's houses and in sight of all that forgotten real estate, along with all the amiable conversations on phones across America and evenings shared in movie houses, around the corner from a recent homicide, down the block from wild lots and weeds, great unknowns, colossal, all evolving along with Darwin and his species. One's life, assumed to be finite, ticking away. Night covers things up but you can still hear the rain.

Pressure comes from a thousand enemies buried in your heart. You practice fighting them, and then one day, it seems like they're gone. One day, allowing for silences, it breaks. You can prepare. It's like preaching. Ready yourself.

HOUSE ON FIRE

House on fire.   Seen before husband.   Just into it.   Resist the
sorrowful bird mother.   Approach forest empty.   Mistake to
think.   Song about stew.   Rig with a bed.   Long season, very hot
for awhile.   Cancer in the family.   Ride up the hill.   Almost as if.

IF ...

If worry were a required human activity, we would all be bald and cowed. We would think twice about even the best things, like seagulls and club sandwiches. Randomness would be eliminated, and we'd be forced to court the favor of the normalizing agencies, which would be manned by actors who couldn't get other work, so they'd be extra-thick believers.

If it were up to me, I'd have special holidays where all public behavior was like the oldest, most respected traditions. And all private behavior would make us immediately handsome.

FOUR UNRELATED SENTENCES WITH UNRELATED ELEMENTS

She exchanged her stupor for a piercing gaze what with the oranges dancing and bungling their routine so perversely.

A jester claimed westward expansion on his tax return and asphixiated on a clogged flute.

There were colors in the sky like green which narrowly missed being eerie.

And it got us nowhere, after all that, so much to the embarrassment of the archangel we just blew it out.

INSTRUCTIONS

Should you ever find a feeling broken and dark, apply bleach
to its forelegs, there by the grainy edge, and hold under cold
water for about a minute. If you let it dry in the window's
natural light, a great glow will fill your heart, like a pearly
munchkin aura beating up on the dark visages of alkie
fuzzies.

Bleat out your trombone when you hear the skinny wailing
from the back of the store. This will ward off any snakes in
the area. But ultimately, when the need arises, there will be
no stopping it. A tiny brightness will appear in the mirror,
slowly rotating around itself, making a moat-like pattern that
will mesmerize and fascinate you. It will be the most interest-
ing thing you have ever seen, and you will not be able to look
away.

Then a sinewy substance will begin to form in the spaces
between you and other water-bearing objects. You will feel
proud and even secure, but then almost without realizing it,
you will have become cut off from everything around you,
and then you will hear her silky voice, the voice of the heart-
eating siren, and she will tell you to bring me to her. Do not
let this happen. Do not come to me at that point. It will be
too late for you, and I am sorry for that, but leave me out of

it. I will be long gone anyway, and I'm not telling you where. If it pretends to thank you, just go along with it. Under that ugliness lies a great sadness, and under the sadness, that's the best place for meat.

Take those tremors that start in the second month of treatment, and blend into a smooth paste. Jam all your jitters into a secret wall box, what the old desert healers used to call a plum pot. Be on the radio. Then when everything seems quiet, call the authorities and demand a hearing. Prepare statements. Hire representatives and expert witnesses. For so many days all efforts must be directed at a single purpose.

When the day arrives, no one will show. It will be the most colossal blow-off of all time. A distant trumpet. The damp fog of dissipated purpose. A few of the guards will seem to be whispering behind your back. Have them fired. Bake muffins.

NEW LOVE I

Spends the whole future drying the dampness made from years of humid suitors. An old way of talking or of being. Sneaks around the shadowy halls while we blank the blank blank house at the what what road, but we had to admit, over our dead bodies might take too long. Inching towards catharsis, brainy moods overtook our lazy hearts, ambling up a narrow path towards our goals: a tree, from the past, still there, no matter what. Then: a dirigible. However unlikely. Stomach contents revealed a nurtured life. And then, look here, say it's blue, say it's worn out, beautiful, say it's new today and noisy, say mighty things. Make fly, leave waste. Sound it out: di-ri-gi-ble. Stony glares from the media gallery. But our spirits were buttressed by the hair and makeup treatment and our new fruit. No native poise so great that it cannot be improved by a mango. Another day, a beach date: walk walk walk walk splash splash flop down quiet then hot and lean in, smooth around the ankle area. Then: hot dogs.

THE DAILY AUDIT

Convey for morons. It's a living. Tending baskets. Pies bleed. Flee above the drainage, it's cleaner. It goes to town with a yellow hat, making sincere dreamlike interpretations of vast swaths of city life for personal enjoyment, as if stoking a huge fire. The air is so wet, I'm bleeding. We bake tomorrow in our fretting juices. What takes its chewing softly? What takes the day and makes it gone?

Sagging police, dropping in the intersections of modernity and obsolescence. Pointing to cards, shaking their heads as if it used to mean something but doesn't mean anything anymore. A hope, like glazed donuts and pies, shining to all equally, except for those imprisoned and others hungry and dying. Again a day anyway. So what makes it?

It comes together when no one's looking, really. It dreams its pies, ready for something, puckered. If you hear a knock, just open it. And then there were the dogs: a mixed breed, a dachshund, a terrier, and a fat lab. We broke bread, spoke quietly of the day's events, they nodded sullenly, and then they were gone. From the roof, I saw something that could have been one of those fake places, made over to look real, but it was only Paris. Me and my big feet.

A tune, aloft, smiled on the night. It takes too many sounds of sand to start your own desert. Please we begged the arm chair, the area rug, the doorjamb, please make it possible. Silence. No one understands. No one even tries. It's comfortable the way cotton is comfortable and meatloaf sandwiches. I'm not making this up.

CONDITIONAL CLAUSES

When the police came
After the juicer gave out
Before orphans placed fifth
As I thought of them as halibut
If Sophie blanched
Where Martha rose
On a sudden bright day
When its manner was praised
As a thick mist ploughed the gorge

CLICK AWAY

A washer pounds away in the basement, prickly static rising from circuits inside an envelope made of folded ether. A bright spot in an otherwise tanked-up song room, with bugs and hot spots and boys invoking bands you never cared about.

Please take calm steps towards the door without protesting. That was what her wall eye seemed to say, staring out at me from a single photo brick in the monstrous plasma screen empire. Please click away. I clicked away.

I took out every reference to boredom and loneliness like they asked me to. My chest was flinching. Angina? Qualms?

A trendiness crept into the atmosphere. It was an orange and blue light flickering on around the house in the dusk. Night can have its own style, without anyone doing anything, I concluded.

I could see flowers through the cars. There's never any diamonds. Rushed lines. A breezy tromp along avenues among neighbors. The evening walk. No assault, no hello. A big, bad finding out. That's all we've got for now, until the all clear.

SYSTEMATIC/SYMPTOMATIC

At the base of a low wall, a colony of rare ants designs itself an unnecessary world. Not squandering, not without a nod from the ancients, not important though either. Backing off, its stillness amplified a sweet, rotting scent, which we later took for the wings shed by a swirl of moths who had decided to become worms again.

If it weren't so meticulously organized, we'd manage to just breathe awhile, where the abstracted feet meet the path. The silence here is the same out on the islands. "That's the whole thing about it," once a sailor said to me. "The whole lot of them produce a certain weight in flowers and then seeds, and silence is the same everywhere." Not true, I thought.

I brought this question to your mother. "When we're heroes," she said, "we later deflate and build tiny guillotines to execute each other repeatedly, but without cruelty. But traveling there," she added, "we meet those peripheral characters who give us all our best ideas. In this way monuments are cruel to life."

THE PATRIOT

When America was still a provincial society, I asked you to dance and you didn't hear. You seemed to be listening to the small population of Shakers in South Eastern Kansas, who doted on you with pies and elegiac sentences.

When America was still a provincial society, a flock of noisy crows bandied about amid morning traffic, goaded by the escalating hostilities among the humans in winter. Terrible barbed wire threw itself over portions of our yard with a hum, hum and a one. If only you had heard me, we could have looked into each others' eyes and bargained for alternate energies, the myriad gifts of our provincial engineers. But you thought you could get around me there behind the barricade, and then the gendarmes took you prisoner, and now here you are barking commands to elephantine captives of the hooting brigades, all because of those damned crows.

A parade broke down on the highway, and floats and marching bands dispersed in the ditches along the road. I tried not to stare at the delicate movements of the brass section trembling before the Veterans of Foreign Wars, but this was, after all, the evolution of the species, and so I could not help getting involved. I walked the parade route by myself, not out of nostalgia, but out of gratitude to all our fortunate bodies dissembling easily in the golden afternoon, which for reasons I never understood I would always think of as "The Afternoon of the Fishes." I wished I could remember your face when you said we took so much for granted when America was still a provincial society.

SECOND PART

PLEDGE OF ALLEGIANCE

I pledge intrepid altitude to the alchemic states of insouciance.

I pledge a penny to each bared bottom.

I pledge smiley candor to the hordes of inept and debased.

I pledge thousands of dust particles slightly altered by sunlight.

I pledge my laundry list in two week intervals.

I pledge apertures opening on afternoons into us and our together smiles.

I pledge restitution to the many calamitous dreamers who tripped over the rug in my foyer.

I pledge a sickly shining caper wrote by genius drunk on whimsy.

I pledge my earnest.

I pledge forgiveness to the stupid moments I might otherwise get hung up on.

I pledge my hats, which I never wear anyway.

I pledge estranged lesbian daughters everywhere.

I pledge allegiance to time and sunlight which accumulate and dissipate continuously whether or not we like each other or even understand each other.

I pledge righteousness in small easily digestible caplets.

I pledge a manic distraction, wrestled with each day, and now and then gloriously defeated.

I pledge the occasional lifting of the veil (and swift being, suddenly in focus, seemingly by truth-telling, duly noted).

NEW LOVE II

Someone baking weeds left out a huge rusty jungle dinner. Hard words pelting strange days. Later agents hung down, breathing porcelain sonnets about lime, marshmallows, and bark. Even her toes are sweeter then, when you get around to them, and you are sweeter for it. A bustle strapped onto a bicycle was very precise. We were crazy about it, for awhile.

THE LIVING SECTION

A city like an attic gets full and neglected. Later it gets mined by imaginative souls caught up in their own futures. Mistakes are always made, but a harmony of furies is observed by sensitive souls, until they are consumed and carried off in waves of dread. We try to sing to them, try their hands on the soft earth in the garden, and this seems to help.

As an experiment I decided that each day I would try to make the shortage of terror seem less arbitrary. So each day I went to the sitting room with its armchair, its ottoman, its divan, and each day I said "I am nothing but vapor condensing around the cool sun. I am nothing but vapor condensing around the cool sun."

The doctor kept saying, "Trying to avoid disease is like dodging raindrops." That is, sometimes it felt like it was working, but you never believed it. The doctor seemed to be made of knowledge, with a thin covering of skin.

"I am nothing but vapor condensing around the cool sun."

Tuesday, Sunday, doesn't matter.

Days passed all change and nothing changed, and the doctor kept pointing to the honey jar. Mad Pooh, we began to call him. Fakey time, in between the furies. I steamed my wrinkled thoughts and they just came out damp and ready to pop back into their old ways. "Go halvsies," said the night ahead.

I was so pleased by talking and singing. I understood that now. My own color was a dye transfer from this day to the next, never quite the same, but always seeming better. Or worse.

CRAP COLLAPSE
ON THE SLOW CHANNEL

out pad out tread out wince the
tidy, a pleasure bargain joined to-
wards its feet
hips together,
like a planned foundling.

A late tunnel thicket takes down
all the ants and the flies and their
coursing, breaks its knees, my
shirt was in shreds it came like
a room in a zone with a mystifier

sling action double-wide
it hits lord
it hits this speed and it's up there with
the mass collapse it's
a mountain city of toad splendor

a cold box of grab-my-legs Kentucky-longs
chief-my-gates-of-autumn
how the farms out there are torn
with ground
it swivels and shrieks

it's hard out there but in here
we're free to grab those gates and
pipe it on in to our own
first season of the shaggy

OLD LOVE I

Do you remember the trundle beds and their voodoo? It was so broad, like that wide river we camped by before everyone knew how to sing so well. It was a time when we risked leaving at the wrong time, going to the wrong place. Well, we never did learn our prayers, did we?

I remember this much: it was our best month of the year. We drank every night, just enough to hear the thunder and move inside. With all the stripes and polka dots settling in around us, we kept our days plain. Then came the winter and we shrank to the size of our belt buckles, our zippers flying under cold fingers, our strange, bright sin.

The forest became a polite grove of trees. My blood became alkaline, my breath became visible, and we became a couple of tramps in fatigues. It broke that. Broke it apart and drove you away.

Later you don't know what we did but I'll tell you now: we broke each other's faces with rash gestures of affection. We thought if we named it all our blankets of the purple night would evaporate, but it's par for the course for now. I have tied my shins together with static, and daily I visit the mountain where we hid the flood. All that's left now is the air above the house and how it puddles in the uneventful weather like mayonnaise.

A BENDFUL OF TONE

lacy regards wound around
a ton just fellated timid
ice wrought in times
like night like tines
of instruments forgiving
us for giving you so much trouble

blended rough hours
made in better days
a ten hut tribute
to scandalous rage
pretended
like children
how we could soldier on
like each other enough
to pretend

and then, when feet assemble
takes pleasure doesn't it in simple texture
crunchy rushes and frog bones
attic sugar and slanted light
a box, becomes you, tends itself
for wintering over
cold laughter drapes itself
foreign fortune
attack a slant of shadow
a mad track vanishing

OBJECTS FOR THE HOME

Adolescent banter pierced the walls like a religious vision, bridging again the gap between the exigencies of the day and the levitation of saints. It sits there yellow and charms us every day, like sunlight on a slow macadam road. Undivided vistas and soft bright compartments suitable for the activity of thinking. You are not thinking about me, of course. That is part of your loveliness.

Flying like a winter sparrow that is too domesticated to enact its true wild nature, a great spiral found its way to your optic nerve, seeing at once the environment of choice and nothing at all. At home, a room for each facet of your personality, facets you didn't even know were there. The youth again, not yet drowning you out, wonders what happened to her hat or her comb or something equally quotidian that has vanished into the ether to produce delightful wisps in clouds south of here. When light draws objects effortlessly, one seems to fly along with it.

When such continuities arise, we either sleep or organize search parties. We cannot tolerate the randomness of light and time. We yell and beat our chests, yell into small, electronic devices, coaxing patterns into being so that we might rest our flagging belief on them, and they might remain as objects: charming, purposeful, sure.

CANNIBALS AND CANOPIES

"I love this landscape," said the host. "The cannibals have all left."

But they had not. There were two left, and they feasted on each other by the light reflected off the swimming pool. The party organizer tactfully worked around them.

"Canopies here, and maybe a torch or two in front, describing a great hall." "We've had a chandelier hanging from a hovercraft," said the contractor. "Noisy but dramatic, a sense of departure."

"Really? Yes, that. Good."

Everything was ready. They sat in contemplation, letting the day get away from them.

The cannibals had finished with extremities, and rolled around each other, gouging hungrily into each other's torsos. "What will we do in the morning?" one asked. They slept, having no answer.

Morning breathed into the canopies like a clock, stamping out the little bits of dark and sleep. The cannibals were finished, bled out. It was a new day.

THE ACTUAL UNIVERSE

Fortune glaring over the actual universe, its intensity blinded, flagged roughly inch by inch like they want to say or wish they'd gotten to before, before anyone noticed, and fraught, fraught with climbing or something toughened from illness, fortune glaring over the actual universe.

The actual universe tough like sand or worship when it's never begot anything but more afternoons and only two goddamn times in her life a danish in a diner.

A danish in a diner and milk, and in later years tea and then coffee with its blue bitterness, something blue sandwiched like a tuna, seared, smeared with coal, blackened, decapitated, assembled like that, like we used to sit outside the church sometimes on the blacktop.

Blacktop in the actual universe its intensity blinded from glaring at some future danish in a diner.

THE LANDLADY
AND THE BOARDER

It came to the landlady's attention that her boarder was talking to himself each night at the window. Her boarder was a wealthy man and did not need to work to earn his keep. "That went out with the war," she thought. She went for onions to the market and asked the grocer about rain. The grocer pulled the landlady close and said, "I see him at the window, too."

THE ORCHESTRA
AND THE WHALE

The orchestra blinks
wonders why when over-tired
whales rise rather than sink
And their voices hum a lot
Their whole outward countenance
goggled with finery as if underwater
keeping one eye on the conductor
one eye on the music
and one eye on the whale

FULL CIRCLE

1. The First Day

IT STARTED on a day when I was left to my own devices, and I decided to go out walking. Along the road I came to a stand of trees with a large, old, royal feeling about them. A boy was there, bouncing against the sky with thoughts like rocket launchers, all firepower, but stuck on the ground in the end. An acid rain began to fall on our fortunes, and since we were around the same height, our fortunes felt intertwined.

My father had always said I'd meet a boy one day, and now here I was meeting one. But he had never said what would happen then, and I sort of hoped the boy would know what to do.

"People have been passing by here since there were people," he said. He had enormous ears but handsome features like a favorite friend of a brother, elapsed in your life over twenty-odd years and now abruptly pointing out historical features in your path. Later, you poured tea without the slightest haste. It was a perfect Sunday in a lifetime of Sundays.

We took the route by the river until we came upon a cabin, where we stayed. It was rough for about a week, but then personalities abated and time stretched out. It was the kind of place where a strange dog might rummage through your garbage, oblivious to your bright moments and your grim nights alike.

There was no task at hand. We waited for emergencies, and wondered about the world out there. We walked to the meadow on the hill to check out the different weather. We both heard a joke on the radio, and we decided this was important. So in between the chores and meals we began putting on jokes. We had limited material, but we made do.

2. Autumn

IT WAS THE season when plants die, but we're expected to just go on living. My chair beat out rhythms only the trees could hear, like a salute to life in an entirely different scale. Cleansed of its greases, its brittle and damp, a dark flower aped the moonlight, humming some unseemly tune. This is just about what it means to be alone, I thought. A clown, a song over there, etc.

We climbed on and on up hills of dogs running circles around our morbid little fantasies. I stuffed his notes in my socks, so I could forget but not lose them. He was the kind who brought you around, making symbols of your eyes. So he could keep them.

One night an offering broke through its shell with great gusto, on fire with its tiny little speed. We broke out in daylight, a chorus of tonsils, but the sauce was thin. The idler's thoughts crept up the trunks of the trees. The night was otherwise unpopulated and damp and I couldn't smell a thing.

3. Circumstances

EACH GATE was the brink of something, waiting to be breached. Something personal made you stand there, made you turn away, before diving, digging up something else. You would not tell me what it was.

It's not as if we didn't have a terrible plan, but we were so busy trying to forget about it we missed the entire day, with its wind and sun, its people bumping up against each other. They all had terrible plans too, thank god.

This was our plan: we had decided we would need some kind of prairie. We sold prairie necklaces at the mall. They were all brown and no one wanted them. I kept my red beads in my pocket. I told myself they were ready for when the time came. It was windy but quiet otherwise, and the horses were still. I asked myself, why me?

We had only begun raising the funds when they got their hands on the land. Out in open trenches, their machines tore at our hearts.

4. The Last Day

THE DAY WAS a full full-time demon. It braided the hairs on its belly. The sun had gone thank god replaced by a howling wind. He creased his ponderous papers ominously, their ink quietly fading. His memories were scorched by certain love possibilities, private rumors that had dissipated, waterlogged after days of longing.

You weren't happy about our sordid fate, I could tell from the deep shadow of your cleft chin. But I knew I would always count those hours among my finest, there without my mountains, my chime laid down on the gravelly dampness, and my snow, now decomposed, plastered on some flatness of worldness.

She told herself she would break out of this eventually. Said if my sand house were pulled apart by indifferent forces, it would still show itself, blanched and frigid-seeming under this cold sun. Not disappeared, not this here, not his.

Finally, with those two chairs up against the sadness of life, my tender thoughts, as my father had called them, unmade me like an empty afternoon.

COMPONENTS

1. Quality Phrases

Taken by surprise against all reason
A relation of tenuous bonds felt historically
Schemes shattered without consideration
Made credible by their seclusion from weather's arbitrary influence

2. Compound Statements

If possibilities are endless, bring me the fatted calf.
If I harrow you in endless dreams, cut me off after two drinks.
I like the thought of you eating yogurt. My supreme taste buds
will one day rule the world ruthlessly.
Suppression breeds extortion, which goes perfectly with your eyes.

TRIPTYCH

I.

The boy had a tangerine crowded into his armpit.
"You're not trying hard enough!"

II.

ape stare
what enormous pauses
happen you
tipped over

this spider has ears
she's happy quiet light

III.

hard rash toy
with it tendons like
oar-made
apple straw

push functions and
their abracadabra

US AND HER

We waited for her in the fine blue light of the quiet room. And it made us think.

"Remember that day when she took her camera and went out on that long walk over by the train tracks where the tires piled up and the brakes on the train were the only thing stopping us from having a total abracadabra kind of wind, sea, and stars kind of a Dionysian meltdown?"

"Yeah, I remember that day. I remember the train stop at that little town that was only half there and how I still thought we preferred each other then. The blossoms crashed in on the milkweed by the road there where she left us. It got dark and she hadn't come back and we started shouting at that moon, yeah, that night by those tracks and her lost and us there, perfection itself."

Her: "I allowed myself eight days to be still and contemplate facets of this aching life. I used the white noise of a fan to cut the glare of silence. Eventually I moved back to the mainland hoping to disappear. Moved back and forth in the blue light between the present and the ever-expanding past, a past that got diffuse and thick and blinded me."

Us: "And so here we are."

A little boy came in, he couldn't stop laughing. He couldn't have said it better. We all remembered. A pure pleasure was waiting inside a shell of chatter.

OLD LOVE II

Strobes in the bathroom, dull sanctions for Mississippi, tender staccato chatter, a world upon you after the tide came up, and not a soul singing, just an oily crow, cancelled appointment, house torn down.

If we had held on, finished the soup, unsullied, were not herded by mistresses behind the walls, we'd think around each other today, a bright child with scrubbed cheeks, and you the answering sort. Hind legs. Some smothering charm lingered, had its appeal, and left.

It's actually getting higher when the thing turns blue and disappears and all the light goes out of her eyes will go out of her eyes just think of it. Opposite the lantern trucks make their noises, and bright heaven tangles its tendrils around our ankles, pleading like a sound does when nobody wants it. It's free, escapes like an ounce of air unattached, like a mouse runs into the room and under the bed for good—well it seems for good, because it's never seen again. Just think of it, and a warm light falls quiet along a love along a lovely afternoon.

THREE LARGE SWOLLEN THINGS
for Blaster

I.

Lingering amidst our
auger brigade
rigged up with fancy
glows a bride
entirely made of cotton

sticks to sin talk
when it wants fed
options evaporate quickly then
like it never lost anything
lint
even
not without a certain inky grace

to be hewn from
huge hounds
in their suckling linens
nesting there like a
gull out of
season

II.

Lope
a gut
rejoinder
gawking
eagle-eyed

speak
where
only
limp-eyed
lumpen
eat
noons

take
heads
if
necessary,
get
sorted

III.

Llllrrrrrrr

Aaaaaaauuuuuur

Rrrrrggggglllll

Gggggggggmmmmmnnn

Ehhhhhhhhhhhhhh

Sssssssssssk

Wooooooooooooo

Ooooooooooommmmmmmm

Lllllllllllliiiiiiiiiiii

Llllllllllllnnnnnn

Eeeeeeeeooooop

Nnnnnnaaaaaaaaa

Tooooooooooo

Hmmmmmmmm

Iiiiiiiiiiiiiiiiiiiiiiiiiiiip

Nnnnnnnk

Gggggggggddddddd

Ssssssssssst

THIRD PART

SHORT FOR HALPERT

Hal got a mushy schmutz stuck under his floorboards, but he bungled a bottle not hid too good, realizing once he done it how it hadn't just been his only chance, but his right hand, wasted fudge rumpled under an Alka-Seltzer. I'm a pigeon! I'm a pigeon! called one of the kids. Beautiful cherub and son of a bitch, Hal wheezed lovingly. We got a damn pigeon for company, and he's the goddamn captain. Nothing doing, Hal snorted, and accompanied his monkey to silent belches.

R & D

Some machines set tasks in motion. Others set their flying motions right with bravery. Then when bravery tries to climb, its girth will render some new object, which we want, an object wanted after being known. With these machines it becomes known. This is a continuous afterthought: climbing, flying, wanting.

There it is. Resembling an ordinary box, we find that we put things in it, chosen things, which we later eat or otherwise insert inside our person and imagine eating. Then it is all new, we are new, (and) the object (is transformed). It is this box which makes it new, so. This box is a machine in this way, climbing, in this way flying in this way wanting.

We want a subject. We are a subject. We want a subject defined properly, and defining will be changing, and therefore like a machine, like a box.

Another object in a box would be, could be glasses. Will we eat the glasses? No, but if there is a machine for glasses we will want them. We want them to define the subject. We put on glasses to see and drink from them. For either this could mean anything, and certainly climbing. And anything could be flying.

Is it bravery or is it thoughtlessness? Maybe it is. One way to find out is to use the machine, which resembles a box.

...

When you place your head in a vase of tulips and place the

vase in the box, you will later find it is as if they had traveled, and traveling is almost altering, when actually nothing new is present. Combinations evoke change. Try it. Something like traveling will happen and you have gone nowhere, so it will seem like a drug or sudden flight. I run the risk of ridicule by sharing this with you. You will see I had no other responsible option, but others will remark these changes in you like having traveled and seen all that is not new and therefore powerful, and they will become frightened by it and they will come after me. It is just like there is nothing they can do about photosynthesis or digestion, although it is harmless it is very powerful. It is never possible to stop. Do not worry.

...

This all comes out of box 2: douser, smilies, patrouchkas, armature, Huguenots, tremblers, peddlers, paddles, amblitages, rendibulars, ontoluminositories, astors, and maps. Inventory is a kind compendium of objects wanted after staving off, or giving up on, a subject.

...

Steps torture boxes, part 2.
It's about timeliness and action.
Steps torture boxes, part 1.
Same thing, only too late.

DAMN PIGEON FOR COMPANY

Plush facial covering
made of cheese
makes mama smile every
time the whistle calls
her back to the alley of
prohibitive excellence.
Lemon ohms make almonds
after ankle hedges bleed
plumb broke.

Out sock
one sock each
lock tack time
like a serious future
in tall socket makers.
what wakes up little creatures
makes up a song
murders ring back and forth
wake the pilot
wake the plunderer
wake the pallbearer
wake me when it's over

Get us up in there so some day
when time begins
our owls will suddenly know
what to say again if we
could only grow avocado
if only don't be so polite
it's killing me

HOMAGE I

Thanks Max Jacob
for holding onto all that
body hair I thought I didn't
want last year because
the house was on fire and we
thought it would rain tomorrow.

Our pastors have always thought highly of you when they were
thinking at all, and otherwise jolly meetings grew timid in your
faun-y presence. Then when you sang me that Broadway hit
in the barn that day I confess I was only pretending to know
how to dance, but you really knew all the chickens by name. So
thanks, Max Jacob, just have the seams drawn up in a diagram
and you can leave the rest to me.

HOMAGE II

I'm letting the clouds run around
she paraphrased
like hogs on a subway
Lots of lawyers like football
but it was never my idea to invite them

We made it be like the climate
and hoped for breezes
Mad tiny gestures like private semaphores
on speed
"We didn't mean to intrude"
said the layers
the lawyers I mean
but you just know they did
Half of all moths want to get closer
the other half is wary

HOMAGE III

My Dear Marcus,

Your experiments with clumsiness and vice have both frightened and inspired me. Since last I wrote, I have been able to design a new ritual choreography aimed at reducing the weight of my head. At first, this had to be done in the water, and at night, when the visibility gravity was at its lowest. By training this way, I have strengthened my passive muscle groups to resist the usual deposits of what you might call wind that have so often lodged in my head at the slightest weather. I have also established a diet of seeds and gelatin, thereby increasing my body's natural ability to expel wind deposits through my pores and follicles.

As you can imagine, my hair has been growing at an extraordinary rate, and this presents the obvious problem of grooming, shedding, and disposing of huge quantities of what is essentially a hazardous material. I have established a hair closet on my property (I hope you understand my need to withhold information on its specific location) where I have been experimenting with the poultice and other compounds to see if it might be rendered inert. I try not to worry about it, but it is clear that one day I will need to move it unless I can devise a method of incineration that doesn't place me or my cat at risk.

Almost as if in preparation for such an event, I have been dreaming about a distant figure, who turns away, or towards us—it's too far to tell—and seems to motion for general attention. We stand, ready to run, but the scent of the mimosas seduces you, lolling in the grass, struggling to resist, struggling to awaken. It was Dad out there, I knew, but didn't want to be the one to say it. He had to stay 500 yards away because of his hearing problem. Everything was horribly amplified and therefore painful to him. I couldn't take it anymore, so I went back to growing trees.

Long actresses blot out the sun. Apologies make it better, but only for a little while. Snacking doesn't help at all. A tree will be a tremendous ally in the later afternoon, when the attack comes and I drag you out behind it. We'll pray with all the ordinary people. It'll be a whole thing.

Faithfully,
M.

IDEA FOR A SONG

Furious to begin, then a ponderous gait, plodding and bowing, an elephant lopes along with the gypsies, either stops in its tracks or falls over a precipice, and Philip Glass passes by in a train, where bells sing and fog horns, and fat skips are joined by the breeze and the big noises of expanding bodies, ballooning over the ocean, over low, mud architecture, like a lazy pre-industrial afternoon. A rock star recounts a life, fingers a series of disremembered scars, while weather-tracking devices argue over a storm. A dolphin picks up radio signals from a quail. Both rush. Sequencing silence with the fractured roll of a ten-ton ice cream truck whose tinny song begins to play itself, distorted with age, with damage, and with wind.

POISON TRAIL

Arsenic, saddled with a guilt complex, exchanged for a side business, chained to a redwood, left in a coal mine.

SOFT PURE PLEASURE

How is it that this is so beautiful?
How is it that this night exists?
How is it that this—

Portions of tired
eggs stewed in lime
bask in the bowl with
the orchids.

It made a soft pure pleasure maker blush.

MEETING

It was a bright soggy night, perplexed and yet undampened with soft thoughts aglow in the brown heights of righteousness. She assembled her gear methodically, but not without pangs of anxiety, for she did not know if there would be anything left for her at the road where her scant meetings were always taking her. A huge number of doubts crowded the business of packing and unpacking her trusted future astonishment. Back where this tender ocean found her, when she was only a barely walking curious thing, alone but for the bears who raised her, gyrating heavens forced upon her as upon all other beings, where stupid timing ruined most intentions before we had even broken even, she points gently to the right of the nice policeman, who, gazing back, found himself as if in a dream, overwhelmed and humbled by the strangeness of life, as evidenced in the huge awkwardness of the figures there on the ice behind him. How could it take so long to pretend such tiny things? Who was that above us blending crimes into memories like nothings, less substantial than even the powder we gave you for the baby? It sings a bit, it clambers. She brought you here, but now you need to find your own reasons to stay, or else move along.

FOGATHON

I.

If my pleasant bellow shudders before you
fly up, make do, skewer your breath
for example or climb a hovering ricket
Another misguided citizen blows bubbles
for gravity
I belong to fog when fog is shrill

II.

Slender rebuttal like splattering silk
Bend its clock, call its pansy mouse,
chew on sucker ice, a gold
sky plant in a world of less gravity,
a glass for seeing the old yard,
a car potion for measuring angles

Touch this split
or loom large and huffy
My quick lid sits fit
It hits
No song, no future
my old story sound
long, draped over the melting
idgit pox

Mix cream
stay out there
stay for the burly
ocean cattle

III.

Spread long float edges
There is room for these
season-stunted angles,
a fifth of which may be folded
for a man named Larry, who
calls himself an "old dog," a "pilot"
A bleach-white afternoon under

masterful sun-made fingers
A pitch for creating
a taxonomic blueprint
to feed the agnostics
with the un-sounded pleasures
of the park-like feeling
you get in some rooms

IN THIS SHAKEN CHAMBER

Spun apart against a blast
a round rambling
almost a mountaineer
Shout out lean deities
up to their cunning in
albetrossed memories

If only tyrants behaved
a little more like foreign agents
At least register
for chrissakes
A blond,
a bound matter for
you and your
agents and
their bleak bound cousins

A very intense assembly
shakes my matter about you
in a smooth buttery shell
for burying with the embers

Come home now. It's just
us, and we remember Finney
We have always held you
all in very high esteem

Revved up for punctuating
the seamen's folly
It hasn't said yet
how light was bouncing
Making a racket of potions
shattered
Blasting out underground
with time and delight over
shards fermenting noisily
in the rushes

Take it all apart for me
We will make new dogs
and salads immersed in
amber calamity or even
a fine thin flute
made from this reedy bone

A paper seed
broken out, bought, mussed
Make a cloud tremor
upon surface tension
Ghost arms appling out,
brought about, fussed
insisted

More to pass massive
likings in jars
Apply sense to
passive matchings

However one lands,
a mile or an hour ago,
in tropics or some
equator heaviness,
among a pride
of crying
Make some air
in this shaken chamber

A PERFECT BEDLAM
for Peter Z.

My long field drains the sky of its open, its air darkening with
you stretching out in it. You gave us muscles we'd never had
before, then before we knew it it was gone, became dreams
tickled by ringing tones in waving birdsong light. How is it out
there with you? A fog blender's got my back, luckily. A toffee,
a tart, a perfect bedlam. A hose splits, it's like a fountain in this
brackish lake my day. Every animate thing becomes you, and
you animate every inanimate thing. We keep breathing because
it's like that living. We keep breathing, but wanting to be with
you again has got us all preparing, for the first time, to stop.
We're making rich beautiful allegories of our breathing by way
of apology, as long as we're here, succumbing to life. We tell
ourselves we're getting there, but this faith is a man-made thing.
A halleluiah with its tender allouette ice, its elegant metals and
its light machines.

BEAR ROUTINE

The small bear gargled, its indolence heating the room like an incubator. Fresh mint scent brought grand schemes to its mind. It rehearsed nightly after a sleep, climbing onto its makeshift stage, constructed of discarded lumber, at the end of the room by the closet. Needing no warm-up, it dove right into its routine, threw its paws about in emotive gestures: despair! determination! surprise! and so on.

The bear was silent. It was working in the pantomime tradition, learned in its vaudeville days. Here in the little room, the bear remembered the greedy producers, who milked starry-eyed actors, bears, and chimps for a dozen shows a week. He remembered the crowd, giddy with the intoxication of the brief leisure of the working classes, pawing at the air, enjoying themselves.

The bear finished for the night just as light broke and a few finches warbled. He shed his muzzle and his nightshirt and opened the door to the day.

PARKED

gallop
lisp
parade
plug

skintight
orange
oily
planet

my phrase
embraces
effortless
placards
which you
bake
into pasture

there was
an hour
a perfect hour
between bells

they argued
over spoons
dark
and trees

OLD LOVE III

Here's to the binderies, the embroideries, the placating, the brocading, the plotting to overrun the wineries. Feelsome juices starched out of their minds each morning, only to explode in the yellow light at noon. Meantime, a sandwich befriends its plate quietly over there in the bright kitchen. Climb through its jellies for you are destined to become a scuba diver. Look how supporting the kids are, how they gather around at suppertime and compare meats. As for me, my eyes ache with indecision, but I leave craving you again, even after all the purses you stole, and our stoves, so filthy with failed soups. Whereas this submarine is so blithely lurking, your torpedo is planning a benefit auction for local squid. So I'll just take a break here in the tall grass. I am counting crickets for something to do, and listening to the flora seed. It is so quiet it is almost not even happening. I'll see you overland, years later. I'll be the one wearing chaps.

Megan McShea lives in Baltimore. She is an archivist
at the Smithsonian Institution.

NOTES

"Crap Collapse on the Slow Channel," "Idea for a Song," "Damn Pigeon for Company," "Fogathon," "In This Shaken Chamber," and "Parked" were all originally written as improvised transcriptions of live, experimental, improvised music, mostly at the Red Room and High Zero festivals in Baltimore, MD.

"11 Irritations That Morning" is the result of re-arranging all of the words in a list I wrote called "13 things I don't want to do alone." The only word that was altered was 13, changed to 11 so that people wouldn't think I was referencing "13 Ways of Looking at a Blackbird" by Wallace Stevens.

In "The Appointment," the dogs that turn into soldiers are from a dream I actually had. In the dream, I died, shot by one of the soldiers. My mother was also in the dream, as she is in the story, but in the dream she was vacuuming.

The "New Loves" and "Old Loves" were all originally untitled pieces. As I began to read them in public, I wanted to give them names, and I realized that one or the other of those two titles suited almost everything I had ever written.

"Pledge of Allegiance" was written after 9/11.

"Three Large Swollen Things" is composed of 3 acrostics of the phrase "large swollen things," which I borrowed from a poem written by Blaster Al Ackerman. The last acrostic is a tribute to a method Blaster once told me he used to respond to telemarketers, in which he basically groans until they hang up.

The Homage poems are humble imitations of Max Jacob (I), Frank O'Hara (II), and Ben Marcus (III).

The policeman referenced in "Meeting"—"overwhelmed and humbled by the strangeness of life"—was inspired by a scene in the movie "Man on Wire" about Philippe Petit, who illegally rigged and crossed a tightrope between the towers of the World Trade Center in 1974. In the movie, there is footage of one of the arresting officers being interviewed at the time, and his awe and wonder at Petit is palpable.

"A Perfect Bedlam" was written in the aftermath of the incomprehensible death of my friend Peter. It documents an actual event that occurred in the days following his death, those days of early grieving when it is difficult to figure out how to be alive, when I went to water the garden on a very hot June day and my hose did split, and a fountain of freezing water drenched me, snapping me out of my grim haze.

ACKNOWLEDGMENTS

The initial compilation of this collection was made during a residency at the Hambidge Center for the Creative Arts and Sciences in Rabun Gap, Georgia in November of 2010.

The following appeared in various issues of *The Shattered Wig*, edited by Rupert Wondolowski:
House on Fire (#22)
Homage I (#21)
The Daily Audit (#25)
New Love I (#28)
Pledge of Allegiance (#21)
The Landlady and the Boarder (#22)
Homage III (#22)

"Objects for the Home" and "Baltimore Prayer" appeared in *On Earth As It Is*. "Sight Unseen"and "A Bendful of Tone" were in the *i.e. reader* and "Instructions" was in *Everyday Genius*. "Meeting" appeared in *Topograph: New Writing from the Carolinas and Beyond*. "Three Large Swollen Things" appeared in WORMSBOOK. "Damn Pigeon for Company" appeared in Blades (#50). "Us and Her" and "Cannibals and Canopies" appeared in a zine that accompanied the 2012 exhibition *Queer is Where the Heart Is*, in Reykjavik, Iceland and Baltimore, Maryland.

The author would like to thank Adam Robinson for his precise, sharp, and thoughtful editing and for all the energy he gave to this book, Stephanie Barber for her cover design and her many unflinching iterations in response to my input, Rupert Wondolowski for his contribution to the back cover, as well as for putting me in print all these years when it never occurred to me to seek publication, without which encouragement I may not have kept writing at all, and finally to Chris Toll for his reliably fearless red pencil.